Colors in My World

Blue in My World

By Brienna Rossiter

level
1
little blue
readers

www.littlebluehousebooks.com

Little Blue House is distributed by North Star Editions:
sales@northstareditions.com | 888-417-0195

Produced for Little Blue House by Red Line Editorial.

Photographs ©: Shutterstock Images, cover, 4, 7, 8–9, 12–13, 15, 16 (top left), 16 (top right), 16 (bottom left), 16 (bottom right); iStockphoto, 11

Library of Congress Control Number: 2020900794

ISBN
978-1-64619-157-4 (hardcover)
978-1-64619-191-8 (paperback)
978-1-64619-259-5 (ebook pdf)
978-1-64619-225-0 (hosted ebook)

Printed in the United States of America
Mankato, MN
082020

About the Author

Brienna Rossiter enjoys playing music, reading books, and drinking tea. She lives in Minnesota.

Table of Contents

I See Blue

I see the ocean.

It is blue.

I see the umbrella.

It is blue.

I see the pail.

It is blue.

I see the tube.

It is blue.

tube

I see the towel.

It is blue.

towel

I see the shoes.

They are blue.

Glossary

pail

tube

towel

umbrella

Index